Sports Illustrated KIDS

BASKETBALL

SHOES, SHORTS, AND STYLE

by Matt Doeden

CAPSTONE PRESS
a capstone imprint

Capstone Captivate is published by Capstone Press, an imprint of Capstone.
1710 Roe Crest Drive
North Mankato, Minnesota 56003
www.capstonepub.com
SPORTS ILLUSTRATED KIDS is a trademark of ABG-SI LLC. Used with permission.

Library of Congress Cataloging-in-Publication Data is available on the Library of Congress website.
ISBN: 978-1-66390-659-5 (library binding)
ISBN: 978-1-66392-069-0 (paperback)
ISBN: 978-1-66390-656-4 (eBook PDF)

Summary: How does basketball players' style on the court affect fans' everyday style choices? In countless ways! From shoes, shorts, and headbands to hairstyles and body art, discover the evolution and influence of basketball fashion both on and off the court.

Image Credits
Associated Press: AP Photo, 5, Marcio Jose Sanchez, 25, Nick Wass, bottom right 7, 21; Getty Images: Andy King, 10, Bryan Bedder, 27, Focus On Sport, middle left 7, Henry Groskinsky, bottom left 9, Kevin C. Cox, 29; Newscom: Laurent VU/SIPA, 26, Phil Masturzo, 19; Shutterstock: Africa Studio, (chalk), design element, Alex Kravtsov, (boys) Cover, Chamnong Inthasaro, (court), design element, ChromaCo, (girl), design element, Dan Thornberg, (basketball texture), design element, EFKS, (arena), back cover, design element, SvgOcean, (word), design element, teka12, (player), design element, vldkont, (ball texture) Cover; Sports Illustrated: Damian Strohmeyer, bottom 7, bottom right 9, 18, Erick W. Rasco, 13, Hy Peskin, top left 7, top right 7, top left 9, John Iacono, top middle 7, top right 9, 11, John W. McDonough, bottom middle 7, 8, 15, 17, 22, Manny Millan, bottom middle 7, 12, 20, 24, Robert Beck, 16, Walter Iooss Jr, 6

All internet sites appearing in back matter were available and accurate when this book was sent to press.

Printed and bound in the United States of America. PO4270

TABLE OF CONTENTS

Words in **bold** are in the glossary.

FABULOUS STYLE

The arena was rocking. The fans were on their feet. The 1991–1992 season marked a new era in the history of the University of Michigan men's basketball team. Five of the nation's top college freshmen stepped onto the court together to take on college basketball. The "Fab Five" had the skills on the court. But they had something more. They had **swagger** and style.

The five young men came onto the court in very long, baggy shorts. That caught everyone's attention. Basketball shorts had always been shorter. Tighter. But not these. Their shorts kicked off a new wave of sports fashion. And the baggy shorts were the style of choice at all levels of basketball for nearly three decades. It was no longer just about playing well. It was about looking good while you did it.

Michigan's "Fab Five" included (left to right) Jimmy King, Juwan Howard, Chris Webber, Jalen Rose, and Ray Jackson.

CHAPTER 1

FASHION ON THE COURT

The Fab Five may have set a **trend** with their baggy shorts. But their style is just one chapter in the history of basketball shorts.

Early basketball shorts were . . . short. And tight. They mostly stayed that way until the 1980s. Then, a new wave of stars began wearing them just a bit longer. They were looser. Less restrictive. Less revealing. The 1990s brought on the ultra-long, baggy style. Men and women embraced it. But by the late 2000s, baggy was out. The shorts got just a bit shorter again.

Larry Bird (#33), sporting typical early 1980s short shorts, takes a shot over Julius Erving (#6).

BASKETBALL SHORTS TIMELINE

1950s

1960s

1970s

1980s

1990s

2000s

2010s

2020s

LeBron James dons his signature Nikes in a 2015 game.

Sweet Kicks

It's all about the shoes. At least that's what many basketball fans and players believe. No piece of basketball fashion is more important. Shoes need to give support, grip, and bounce. But they also have to look *good*.

Until the 1970s, the Converse Chuck Taylor was the shoe of choice. But then, a wave of new shoes changed the scene. The biggest of them was the Nike Air Jordan. It came out in 1985. The sleek, stylish shoes changed the market, on and off the court. Michael Jordan was the biggest star in basketball. And his shoes were iconic. Reebok pumps were all the rage in the early 1990s. Nike, Adidas, and Under Armour shoes dominate the modern game.

BASKETBALL SHOES TIMELINE

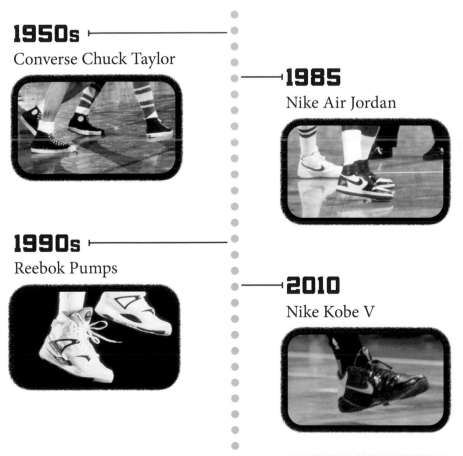

1950s
Converse Chuck Taylor

1985
Nike Air Jordan

1990s
Reebok Pumps

2010
Nike Kobe V

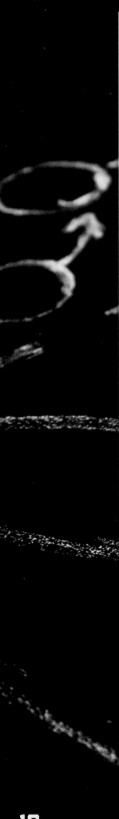

Accessorize!

On-the-court fashion doesn't stop with uniforms and shoes. Players have always added their own personal flair with **accessories**.

Wilt Chamberlain helped make headbands popular. Cliff Robinson, Candace Parker, and LeBron James all made the headband part of their style. Goggles and wristbands also added a personal touch. And who could forget high socks? Elliot "Socks" Perry got his nickname and basketball identity from his high socks. It's a signature style that's not for everyone. But when it works, it works.

Candace Parker rocks her headband during a WNBA Finals game against the Minnesota Lynx.

Kareem Abdul-Jabbar (#33) wears his trademark goggles as he battles for position near the basket.

CHAPTER 2

PERSONAL TOUCH

Style doesn't stop with clothes. A player's entire appearance can be a fashion statement. And for many, it starts with the hair.

In the 1990s, Dennis Rodman was almost as famous for his hair as he was for his basketball skill.

The **Afro** has been a staple of the National Basketball Association (NBA) for decades. From Dr. J to Ben Wallace, the Afro is a statement in big hair. Allen Iverson's cornrows and Brittney Griner's dreadlocks helped set new standards for style. Ricky Rubio's man bun, Michael Jordan's shaved head, and Sue Bird's ponytail all helped make their mark on the style of the game. And Dennis Rodman had a style all his own. His brightly colored hairstyles changed often. And they were *never* boring!

Brittney Griner (#15) plays against Spain in the 2016 Summer Olympic Games.

Well-Groomed

For men, hairstyle doesn't end with the head. Facial hair can be every bit as important to a player's look.

James Harden is one of the greatest players in history. But he's just as well known for his beard. It's quite a beard! In college, Harden played clean-shaven. But when he hit the NBA, he came with a new look. Harden started growing his beard in 2009. He's had it ever since!

Of course, he's not alone. Bill Russell, Kareem Abdul-Jabbar, and Kevin Love have all sported amazing beards. And Drew Gooden's braided beard was truly one of a kind.

"The Beard," James Harden, gets his nickname from his bushy facial hair.

Got Ink?

Some style choices are forever. In recent decades, tattoos have become a big part of basketball culture. Dennis Rodman and Allen Iverson helped make body art popular. Now, it's everywhere. Crosses, phrases, and wild beasts cover the skin of many basketball players.

Kobe Bryant had "Vanessa"—his wife's name— tattooed on his arm. Cappie Pondexter has the Women's National Basketball Association (WNBA) logo. Seimone Augustus has a **sleeve** of flowers on her right arm.

Seimone Augustus (#5) shows off her sleeve of tattoos in a game for Team USA.

Chris "Birdman" Andersen set a new standard for tattoos in the NBA. He completed this punk style with a wild mohawk hairstyle.

BIRDMAN

Chris "Birdman" Andersen has some of the most famous tattoos in basketball. Andersen's many tattoos include wings on his arms and the words *FREE BIRD* on his neck. With his body art, wild hairstyles, and above-the-rim game, Andersen set a new standard for the punk style in the NBA.

Miami's Dwyane Wade performs his pregame ritual, doing pull-ups on the rim.

CHAPTER 3

EXPRESSION ON THE COURT

Style is about more than looks. It's about attitude. *Swagger.* Every player has his or her own way of showing their personality. It helps get them amped up. And the fans love it.

Rituals are a big part of it. LeBron James tosses chalk into the air before each game. Steph Curry shoots the ball from the locker room tunnel. Before he retired, Dwyane Wade did pull-ups on the rim.

Poof! A cloud of chalk dust floats through the air after LeBron James's famous pregame ritual.

Signature Moves

It takes a special player to make a signature move. Kareem Abdul-Jabbar had his famous skyhook. He would rise up and fling the ball over his head and into the net. Dominique Wilkins threw down amazing tomahawk dunks. He'd soar through the air and slam the ball down hard with one hand. Hakeem Olajuwon froze defenders with his Dream Shake. Maya Moore's spin move left defenders in the dust.

Kareem Abdul-Jabbar's signature skyhook was almost impossible to defend.

Elena Delle Donne (#11) fires a step-back jumper over Natasha Howard.

The list goes on. Earvin "Magic" Johnson was the master of the no-look pass. Elena Delle Donne and Dirk Nowitzki perfected the **fadeaway** jump shot. Each player's signature move became part of their style.

Celebrate!

Swish! How does a player celebrate big shots and plays? For many, it's just a shrug. But others have their own unique ways to pat themselves on the back.

Dikembe Mutombo was a shot-blocking machine. And he'd let opponents know about it. He used his famous finger wag. It was his way of reminding them not to try to shoot over him. Steph Curry celebrated big three-pointers by tapping his chest and pointing to the sky. Jason Terry would stick out his arms like wings and jet back up the court.

Jason Terry (left) jets up the court after knocking down a shot.

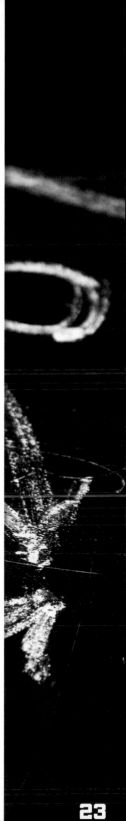

CHAPTER 4

FASHION, CULTURE, AND SOCIAL ISSUES

Shoppers line up for a chance to buy Nike Air Jordans in 2011.

Style doesn't stop on the court. NBA fashion is a part of popular culture. Air Jordan shoes are not just for basketball. They are a fashion statement. People line up to buy the new release each year. Basketball jerseys have become staples in hip-hop fashion. Some NBA fans even get tattoos like the ones their favorite players have.

Looking Good

Fashion is important to many players off the court. Designer suits, wild hats, and slick shoes help each player develop a style.

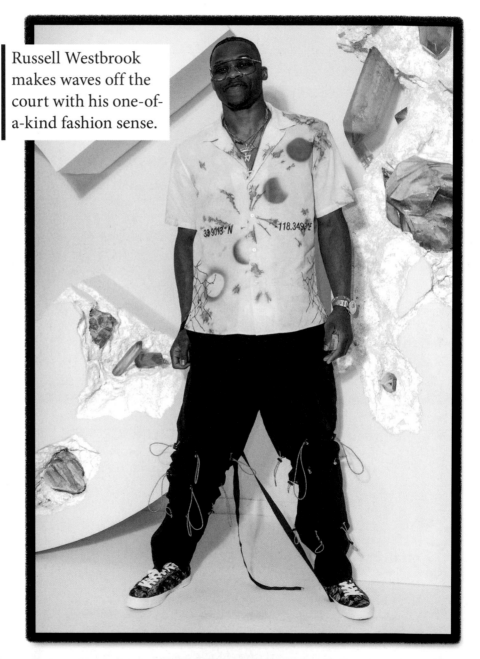

Russell Westbrook makes waves off the court with his one-of-a-kind fashion sense.

For many, a basic black suit is enough. But others dress to stand out. Russell Westbrook is a fashion trendsetter. His unusual combinations and bright colors keep people watching. The WNBA's Tamera Young has her own sense of style. It often includes designer clothing paired with bright sneakers. Swin Cash wows with sleek, elegant dresses.

Swin Cash shows off her sense of style in a blue evening gown at an event.

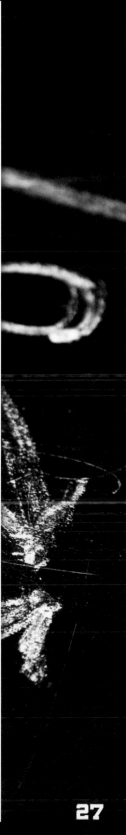

Style Sends a Message

In recent years, NBA and WNBA players have used fashion as a way to speak out on issues. In 2020, **social justice** was on many players' minds. Police shootings of Black people left some players wanting to speak out. Many NBA players wore the words *Black Lives Matter* on their jerseys.

The WNBA got involved too. Their warm-up shirts honored Breonna Taylor with the phrase *Say Her Name*. Taylor was shot and killed by police in March 2020. It was a small way that players could stand up for their beliefs and spread a message of change.

Players kneeled together before a 2020 NBA game. They wore T-shirts to raise awareness about social justice issues.

GLOSSARY

accessory (ak-SEH-suh-ree)—a stand-alone item that helps complete a style or look

Afro (AFF-roh)—a curly hairstyle in which the hair stands out all around the head

fadeaway (FAYD-a-way)—a shot taken while a player jumps, or fades, away from the rim

signature (SIG-nuh-chur)—something that sets a person apart and identifies them

sleeve (SLEEV)—a tattoo or series of tattoos that cover a person's arm

social justice (SOH-shuhl JUHSS-tiss)—the idea that society should treat all people equally and fairly

swagger (SWAG-uhr)—a highly confident way of looking and behaving

trend (TREND)—a popular movement toward a style or idea

READ MORE

Mattern, Joanne. *What It Takes to Be a Pro Basketball Player.* Mankato, MN: 12 Story Library, 2020.

Pryor, Shawn. *Basketball's Most Ridonkulous Dunks!* North Mankato, MN: Capstone, 2021.

Velasco, Catherine Ann. *Behind the Scenes of Pro Basketball.* North Mankato, MN: Capstone, 2019.

INTERNET SITES

NBA
nba.com/

SIKids Basketball
sikids.com/basketball

WNBA
wnba.com/

INDEX